Great Thinkers

A Collection of Wise Words

DAVID ADEYANJU

ISBN: 147009228X
ISBN-13: 978-1470092283

DEDICATION

This book is dedicated to the loving memory of my mother

CONTENTS

ACKNOWLEDGMENTS

Special thanks to my editor Sharon Kemi a lady of great patience and understanding, without whom this work would not have been this possible.

FOREWORD

Our world and way of life is changing, and as we all know, change is the only constant thing in life. One major motivation for change is the quest to do things better, smarter and faster.

Therefore, we cannot afford to go through this life the same way the generations before us did, we must ensure we learn from their mistakes and apply the learning in our daily life endeavours, so that we can avoid some of their mistakes, and leverage on their strength to in turn do things in a much better and smarter way.

It is my sincere desire that as many as will read this book, will gain wisdom from the wise words of these great leaders, achievers, philosophers and visionaries and apply them as it affects every facet of their life's.

CHAPTER ONE

Discipline is the bridge between goals and accomplishment.

- Jim Rohn, American Businessman, Author, Speaker, Philosopher

It is far more impressive when others discover your good qualities without your help.

-Judith Martin/Miss Manners

Beware of little expenses. A small leak will sink a great ship.

-Benjamin Franklin, 1706-1790, American Scientist, Publisher, Diplomat

You will either step forward into growth or you will step back into safety.

-Abraham Maslow, 1908-1970, American Psychologist

You might well remember that nothing can bring you success but yourself.

- Napoleon Hill 1883-1970, American Speaker, Motivational Writer, "Think
and Grow Rich

It is not enough to be busy, so are the ants. The question is, 'What are we busy about?'

-Henry David Thoreau, 1817-1862, American Essayist, Poet, Naturalist

I not only use all the brains that I have, but all that I can borrow.

-Woodrow Wilson, 1856-1924, Twenty-eighth President of the USA

If Columbus had turned back, no one would have blamed him. Of course, no one would have remembered him either.

-Source Unknown

If you conduct yourself as though you expect to be successful and happy, you will seldom be disappointed.

-Brian Tracy, American Trainer, Speaker, Author, Businessman

The reason why worry kills more people than work is that more people worry than work.

-Robert Frost, 1875-1963, American Poet

You never achieve real success unless you like what you are doing.

-Dale Carnegie {1888-1955 American Author & Achievement Expert}

Great ambition is the passion of a great character. Those endowed with it may perform very good or very bad acts. All depends on the principals which direct them.

-Napoleon Bonaparte, 1769-1821, French General, Emperor

A ship in harbor is safe -- but that is not what ships are for.

- John A. Shedd

Never tell people how to do things. Tell them what to do and they will surprise you with their ingenuity.

-General George S. Patton, 1885-1945, American Army General during World War II

What this power is, I cannot say. All I know is that it exists...and it becomes available only when you are in that state of mind in which you know EXACTLY what you want...and are fully determined not to quit until you get it.

- *Alexander Graham Bell, 1847-1922, British-born American Inventor of Telephone*

Patience is not passive; on the contrary, it is active; it is concentrated strength.

-Edward G. Bulwer-Lytton, 1803-1873, British Novelist, Poet

People deal too much with the negative, what is wrong.... Why not try and see positive things, to just touch those things and make them bloom.
-Thich Nhat Hanh, Vietnamese Buddhist Monk, Teacher

At the age of 20, we don't care what the world thinks of us; at 30, we worry about what it is thinking of us; at 40, we discover that it wasn't thinking of us at all.

– *Unknown*

The greatest pleasure I know is to do a good action by stealth, and to have it found out by accident.

-Charles Lamb, 1775-1834, British Essayist, Critic

Lack of forgiveness causes almost all of our self-sabotaging behavior.
-Mark Victor Hansen, American Motivational Speaker, Author

Stop going with the flow in your life. Start your own river instead

.-Dr. Phil, Phillip C. McGraw (1950 -)

There is no security on this Earth, there is only opportunity.
-General Douglas MacArthur, 1880-1964, American Army General in WW II

The most damaging phrase in the language is: "It's always been done that way.

" *-Rear Admiral Grace Hopper*

You cannot teach a man anything; you can only help him find it within himself.

-Galileo, 1564-1642, Italian Astronomer, Mathematician

No one's head aches when he is comforting another.

- Indian Proverb

Before you build a better mousetrap, it helps to know if there are any mice out there. –

-Mortimer B. Zuckerman

There's no scarcity of opportunity to make a living at what you love. There is only a scarcity of resolve to make it happen.

-Wayne Dyer, 1940-, American Psychotherapist, Author, Lecturer

Take your life in your own hands and what happens? A terrible thing: no one is to blame.

-Erica Jong, 1942-, American Author

Excellence means when a man or a woman asks of himself more than others do. –

-Ortega Y Gasset, 1883-1955, Spanish Essayist, Philosopher

Written in Chinese, the word crisis, is composed of two characters. One represents danger and the other represents opportunity.
-John F. Kennedy,1917-1963, Thirty-fifth President of the USA

The nearest way to glory is to strive to be what you wish to be thought to be."

-Socrates {BC 469-399 Greek Philosopher}

-Always work from a list. Write it out, organize it, and work on your most important task.

- Brian Tracy, American Trainer, Speaker, Author, Businessman

Never give in -- never, never, never, never.

-- *Winston Churchill, 1874-1965, British Statesman, Prime Minister*

It is a fine thing to have ability, but the ability to discover ability in others is the true test.

-Elbert Hubbard, 1859-1915, American Author, Publisher

All results no matter how magnificent are infinitesimal when compared to
future possibility.

- James A. Ray

"The world would have you agree with its dismal dream of limitation. But the light would have you soar like the eagle of your sacred visions. -
-Alan Cohen, Author, The Dragon Doesn't Live Here Anymore: Loving Fully, Living Freely

When you judge another, you do not define them, you define yourself.
-Wayne Dyer, 1940-, American Psychotherapist, Author, Lecturer

The secret of success is making your vocation your vacation.

- Mark Twain, 1835-1910, American Humorist, Writer

Success is neither magical nor mysterious. Success is the natural consequence of consistently applying the basic fundamentals.

- Jim Rohn, American Businessman, Author, Speaker, Philosopher

The only free cheese is in the mousetrap.

- Russian Proverb

We attract people into our lives because there is something we need to learn.

- Mary T. Browne

All desires come with some form of risk. NO RISK – NO REWARD!

- Dr. Robert Anthony

It has been said that our anxiety does not empty tomorrow of its sorrow, but only empties today of its strength.

" --Charles Haddon Spurgeon

Everything that irritates us about others can lead us to an understanding of ourselves.

-- Carl Jung, 1875-1961, Swiss Psychiatrist

Success is not to be pursued; it is to be attracted by the person you become.

- *Jim Rohn, American Businessman, Author, Speaker, Philosopher*

When you get to the end of your rope, tie a knot and hang on.

- *Franklin D. Roosevelt, 1858-1919, Twenty-sixth President of the USA*

My goal is simple. It is complete understanding of the universe, why it as it is and why it exists as all.

- *Stephen Hawking, 1942-, British Theoretical Physicist*

Destiny is not a matter of chance, but of choice. Not something to wish for, but to attain.

- *William Jennings Bryan, 1860-1925, American Lawyer, Politician*

Learn to self-conquest, persevere thus for a time, and you will perceive very clearly the advantage which you gain from it.

- *St. Teresa of Avila, 1515-1582, Spanish Saint, Mystic*

Laziness may appear attractive, but work gives satisfaction.

- *Anne Frank, 1929-1945, German Jewish Refugee, Diarist*

In the practice of tolerance, one's enemy is the best teacher.

-*Dalai Lama, 1935-, Tibet Religious Leader Resides In India*

Life is a great big canvas, and you should throw all the paint you can on it.

-Danny Kaye, 1913-1987, American Stage, Film, Television Entertainer

We must all suffer one of two things: the pain of discipline or the pain of regret or disappointment.

 -- Jim Rohn, American Businessman, Author, Speaker, Philosopher

I am always busy, which is perhaps the chief reason why I am always well.
- Elizabeth Cady Stanton, 1815-1902, American Social Reformer and Women's
Suffrage Leader

Success is the child of drudgery and perseverance. It cannot be coaxed or
bribed; pay the price and it is yours.

 -Orison Swett Marden, 1850-1924, American Author, Founder of Success Magazine

I am beginning to learn that it is the sweet, simple things of life which are the real ones after all.

 - *Laura Ingalls Wilder, Author "Little House"*

The reason why worry kills more people than work is that more people worry than work.

-Robert Frost, 1875-1963, American Poet

Doubt whom you will, but never yourself.

 - *Christian Nevell Bovee 1820-1904, American Author, Lawyer*

Making a success of the job at hand is the best step toward the kind you want.

 - Bernard M. Baruch, 1870-1965, American Financier

I like living. I have sometimes been wildly, despairingly, acutely miserable, racked with sorrow, but through it all I still know quite certainly that just to be alive is a grand thing.

-Agatha Christie, 1891-1976, British Mystery Writer

Have something to say, and say it as clearly as you can. That is the only secret of style.

 - *Matthew Arnold, 1822-1888, British Poet, Critic*

Abundance is not something we acquire. It is something we tune into.
-*Wayne Dyer, 1940-, American Psychotherapist, Author, Lecturer*

I shall adopt new views as fast as they shall appear to be true views.
-*Abraham Lincoln, 1809-1865, Sixteenth President of the USA*

Discipline is the foundation upon which all success is built. Lack of discipline inevitably leads to failure.

- *Jim Rohn, American Businessman, Author, Speaker, Philosopher*

The virtue of man ought to be measured, not by his extraordinary exertions, but by his everyday conduct.

-Blaise Pascal, 1623-1662, French Scientist, Religious Philosopher

The path to success is to take massive, determined action.

- *Anthony Robbins, 1960-, American Author, Speaker, Peak Performance Expert /
Consultant*

CHAPTER TWO

Problems are only opportunities in work clothes.

 - Henry J. Kaiser, 1882-1967, American Industrialist

One of the greatest pieces of economic wisdom is to know what you do not know

.-John Kenneth Gilbraith, American Economist

The world is filled with willing people; some willing to work, the rest willing to let them.

 - Robert Frost, 1875-1963, American Poet

There is in every true woman's heart a spark of heavenly fire, which lies dormant in the broad daylight of prosperity, but which kindles up, and beams and blazes in the dark hour of adversity.

 -Washington Irving, 1783-1859, American Author

In business, you don't get what you deserve, you get what you negotiate.

-   *Chester L. Karrass, Author*

Millions saw the apple fall, but Newton was the one who asked why.

-Bernard M. Baruch, 1870-1965, American Financier

There is real magic in enthusiasm. It spells the difference between mediocrity and accomplishment.

- Norman Vincent Peale, 1898-1993, American Christian Reformed Pastor, Speaker, Author

The important thing is not to stop questioning. Curiosity has its own reasons for existing. One cannot help but be in awe when he contemplates the mysteries of eternity, of life, of the marvelous structure of reality

.- Albert Einstein, 1879-1955, German-born American Physicist

It is the peculiar quality of a fool to perceive the faults of others and to forget his own. –

-Marcus T. Cicero, 106 BC - 43 BC, Great Roman Orator and Politician

Experience is a revelation in the light of which we renounce our errors of youth for those of age.

- Ambrose Bierce, 1842-1914, American Author/Editor/Journalist

In every walk with nature one receives far more than he seeks.

- John Muir, 1838-1914, Environmentalist and Naturalist

Chance is always powerful. Let your hook be always cast; in the pool where you least expect it, there will be a fish.

- Ovid, 43 BC - 17 AD, Roman Poet

Don't be afraid to go out on a limb. That's where the fruit is.

- Source Unknown

Good ideas and innovations must be driven into existence by courageous patience.

- Hyman G. Rickover, 1900-1986, Naval Engineering Officer

A wise man should have money in his head, but not in his heart.

- Jonathan Swift, 1667-1745, English Essayist/Novelist/Satirist

Faced with crisis, the man of character falls back on himself. He imposes his own stamp of action, takes responsibility for it, makes it his own. -
-Charles de Gaulle, 1890-1970, French General and Politician

Love is supreme and unconditional; like is nice but limited.

 - *Duke Ellington, 1899-1974, American Jazz Composer, Pianist and Bandleader*

It is understanding that gives us an ability to have peace. When we understand the other fellow's viewpoint, and he understands ours, then we can sit down and work out our differences.

 - *Harry S. Truman, 1884-1972, 33rd President of the United States*

Watch what people are cynical about, and one can often discover what they lack.

 - *George S. Patton, 1885-1945, American Army General during World War II*

The only limit to our realization of tomorrow will be our doubts of today. Let us move forward with strong and active faith.

 - *Franklin D. Roosevelt, 1882-1945, 32nd President of the United States*

People never improve unless they look to some standard or example higher or better than themselves.

 - *Tryon Edwards, 1809-1894, American Theologian*

The tougher the times, the more clarity you gain about the difference between what really matters and what you only pretend to care about.

 - Po Bronson, Best-Selling Author of "What Should I Do With My Life?"

A good heart is better than all the heads in the world.

- Edward G. Bulwer-Lytton, 1803-1873, British Novelist and Poet

Outside of a dog, a book is man's best friend. Inside of a dog, it's too dark to read. –

-Groucho Marx, 1890-1977, American Comedian

Teachers open the door but you must walk through it yourself.

- Chinese Proverb

A true friend is someone who thinks that you are a good egg even though he knows that you are slightly cracked.

- Bernard Meltzer, American Law Professor

Enthusiasm is a telescope that yanks the misty, distant future into the radiant, tangible present.

 - Source Unknown

There is no waste of time in life like that of making explanations.

-Benjamin Disraeli, 1804-1881, British Statesman and Prime Minister

Courtesy is the one coin you can never have too much of or be stingy with.

- John Wanamaker, 1838-1922, American Merchant

Mediocrity knows nothing higher than itself, but talent instantly recognizes genius. - --

- Arthur Conan Doyle, 1859-1930, British Author known for the Sherlock Holmes stories

If opportunity doesn't knock, build a door.

- Milton Berle, 1908-2002, American Comedian known as "Uncle Miltie"

A woman is like a tea bag - you can't tell how strong she is until you put her in hot water.

- Nancy Reagan, Former First Lady of the United States

One can endure sorrow alone, but it takes two to be glad.

- Elbert Hubbard, 1859-1915, American Author and Publisher

Money was never a big motivation for me, except as a way to keep score. The real excitement is playing the game.

 - *Donald Trump, American Businessman and Star of "The Apprentice"*

Part of the secret of success in life is to eat what you like and let the food fight it out inside.

 - *Mark Twain, 1835-1910, American Writer and Humorist*

So much of what is best in us is bound up in our love of family, that it remains the measure of our stability because it measures our sense of loyalty. All other pacts of love or fear derive from it and are modeled upon it.

- *Haniel Long, 1888-1956, American Author/Poet/Journalist*

People of humor are always in some degree people of genius.

 - *Samuel Taylor Coleridge, 1772-1834, British Poet/Critic/Philosopher*

Get action. Seize the moment. Man was never intended to become an oyster.
- *Theodore Roosevelt, 1858-1919, 26th President of the United States*

Education is hanging around until you've caught on.

 - *Robert Frost, 1875-1963, American Poet*

Ninety-nine percent of the failures come from people who have the habit of making excuses.

- George Washington Carver, 1864-1943, American Botanist

It's not what you take but what you leave behind that defines greatness. -
-Edward Gardner, American Businessman and Founder of Soft Sheen Products

An education isn't how much you have committed to memory, or even how much
you know. It's being able to differentiate between what you do know and what you don't.

- Anatole France, 1844-1924, French Novelist

We are what we repeatedly do; excellence, then, is not an act but a habit.
- Aristotle,BC 384-322, Greek Philosopher

I have yet to find the man, however exalted his station, who did not do better work and put forth greater effort under a spirit of approval than under a spirit of criticism.

- Charles M Schwab, 1862-1939, American Industrialist, Businessman

We are hungry for more; if we do not consciously pursue the More, we create less for ourselves and make it more difficult to experience More in life.

 - *Judith Wright, Author, There Must Be More Than This*"

Try not to become a man of success but rather try to become a man of value.

- *Albert Einstein, 1879-1955, German-born American Physicist*

"Persistent people begin their success where others end in failure."
-Edward Eggleston, American Writer, Historian

Do not be too timid and squeamish about your actions. All life is an experiment.

-- *Ralph Waldo Emerson*

Truth is like the sun. You can shut it out for a time, but it's not going to go away.

-- *Elvis Presley*

We all get report cards in many different ways, but the real excitement of what you're doing is in the doing of it. It's not what you're gonna get in the end - it's not the final curtain - it's really in the doing it, and loving what I'm doing.

-- *Designer Ralph Lauren*

Following the way isn't all that difficult; you just have to avoid continually pitting one thing against the other, 'this' against 'that,' and thereby fragmenting the world into opposites.

-- Seng T'san

Trials, temptations, disappointments -- all these are helps instead of hindrances, if one uses them rightly. They not only test the fibre of a character, but strengthen it. Every conquered temptation represents a new fund of moral energy. Every trial endured and weathered in the right spirit makes a soul nobler and stronger than it was before.

-- James Buckham

Face your deficiencies and acknowledge them; but do not let them master you. Let them teach you patience, sweetness, insight.

-- Helen Keller (1880-1968) American Writer

Great minds can sometimes guess the truth before they have either the evidence or arguments for it (Diderot called it having the "esprit de divination"). What do you believe is true even though you cannot prove it?

-Anonymous

The gem cannot be polished without friction, nor man perfected without trials.

-- Chinese proverb

When I went to Montgomery as a pastor, I had not the slightest idea that I would later become involved in a crisis in which non-violent resistance would be applicable. I neither started the protest nor suggested it. I simply responded to the call of the people for a spokesman.

" *-- Dr. Martin Luther King, Jr. (From Stride Toward Freedom)*

It is not the number of books you read, nor the variety of sermons you hear, nor the amount of religious conversation in which you mix, but it is the frequency and earnestness with which you meditate on these things till the truth in them becomes your own and part of your being, that ensures your growth.

-- Frederick Robertson

There are no shortcuts to any place worth going.

-- Beverly Sills

We attract people into our lives because there is something we need to learn."
-- Mary T. Browne

Let us move on, and step out boldly, though it be into the night, and we can scarcely see the way.

-- Charles B. Newcomb

He has half the deed done who has made a beginning.

- Horace, 65-8 B.C., Italian Poet

Don't throw away the old bucket until you know whether the new one holds water.

- Swedish Proverb

CHAPTER THREE

Focus on remedies, not faults.

 - *Jack Nicklaus, American Golfer*

A hug is like a boomerang--you get it back right away.

 - *Bil Keane*, American Cartoonist and Creator of the "Family Circus" comic strip

The world of reality has its limits; the world of imagination is boundless.

- *Jean Jacques Rousseau, 1712-1778, Swiss-born Philosopher/Writer/Political Theorist*

The welfare of each is bound up in the welfare of all.

- Helen Keller, 1880-1968, American Blind/Deaf Author and Lecturer

Histories make men wise; poets, witty; the mathematics, subtle; natural philosophy, deep; moral, grave; logic and rhetoric, able to contend. -
-Francis Bacon, 1561-1626, British Philosopher/Essayist/Statesman

Music expresses that which cannot be said and on which it is impossible to
be silent.

- Victor Hugo, 1802-1885, French Poet/Dramatist/Novelist

Creativity involves breaking out of established patterns in order to look at things in a different way.

- Edward de Bono, Maltese-born Psychologist and Authority on Creative Thinking

Forget injuries, never forget kindnesses.

- Confucius, 551-479 B.C., Chinese Ethical Teacher and Philosopher

If an idea's worth having once, it's worth having twice.

- Tom Stoppard, British Dramatist and Screenwriter

Among its other benefits, giving liberates the soul of the giver.

- *Maya Angelou, American Poet and Writer*

The mode by which the inevitable comes to pass is effort.

- *Oliver Wendell Holmes, 1809-1894, American Author and Poet*

The mind has exactly the same power as the hands; not merely to grasp the world, but to change it.

- *Colin Wilson, English Author*

Security is when I'm very much in love with somebody extraordinary who loves me back.

- *Shelley Winters, American Actress*

Life isn't a matter of milestones, but of moments.

- *Rose Kennedy, 1890-1995, Matriarch of the prominent Kennedy family of the United States*

It's hard to beat a person who never gives up.

- *Babe Ruth, 1895-1948, Hall of Fame American Baseball Player*

You have got to discover you, what you do, and trust it.

– *Barbra Streisand, American Actress and Singer*

It's not the load that breaks you down, it's the way you carry it.

– *Lena Horne, American Singer and Actress*

Forget the times of your distress, but never forget what they taught you.
- *Herbert Gasser, 1888-1963, American Physiologist and Nobel Prize Winner*
for Medicine

When the character of a man is not clear to you, look at his friends.
-
-*Japanese Proverb*

Ultimately, the only power to which man should aspire is that which he exercises over himself.

- *Elie Wiesel, Romanian-born Activist and Novelist*

Honor lies in honest toil.

- *Grover Cleveland, 1837-1908, 22nd and 24th President of the United States*

The way you overcome shyness is to become so wrapped up in something that you forget to be afraid.

- *Lady Bird Johnson, Former First Lady of the United States*

Fast is fine, but accuracy is everything.

- Wyatt Earp 1848-1929, American Gambler/Gunfighter/Lawman

Parents learn a lot from their children about coping with life.

- Muriel Spark, British Novelist

There is no pillow so soft as a clear conscience.

- French Proverb

It isn't a calamity to die with dreams unfulfilled, but it is a calamity not to dream. —

-Benjamin E. Mays, 1895-1984, *American Educator and Clergyman*

There is a time for departure even when there's no certain place to go. -
-Tennessee Williams, 1911-1983, Noted Playwright and Pulitzer Prize Winner

They who dream by day are cognizant of many things which escape those who dream only by night.

- Edgar Allan Poe, 1809-1849, Nineteenth Century Poet/Novelist/Short Story Writer

Baseball is the only field of endeavor where a man can succeed three times out of ten and be considered a good performer.

- Ted Williams, 1918-2002, Hall of Fame Baseball Player for the Boston Red Sox

Everything is okay in the end. If it's not okay, then it's not the end.
-
-Origin Unknown

The greatest of faults, I should say, is to be conscious of none.

- Thomas Carlyle, 1795-1881, Scottish Author/Essayist/Historian

A vacation is over when you begin to yearn for your work.

- Morris Fishbein, 1889-1976, American Physician/Writer/Journal Editor

A talent somewhat above mediocrity, shrewd and not too sensitive, is more likely to rise in the world than genius.

- Charles Horton Cooley, 1864-1929, American Sociologist

Health is the greatest gift, contentment the greatest wealth, faithfulness the best relationship.

- Buddha, 568 BC - 488 BC, Founder of Buddhism

There are incalculable resources in the human spirit, once it has been set free.

- *Hubert H. Humphrey, 1911-1978, American Democratic Politician and Former Vice President of the United States*

A hug is like a boomerang--you get it back right away.

- *Bil Keane, American Cartoonist and Creator of the "Family Circus" comic strip*

The world of reality has its limits; the world of imagination is boundless.

- *Jean Jacques Rousseau, 1712-1778, Swiss-born Philosopher/Writer/Political Theorist*

He has half the deed done who has made a beginning.

- *Horace, 65-8 B.C., Italian Poet*

Don't throw away the old bucket until you know whether the new one holds water.

- *Swedish Proverb*

The welfare of each is bound up in the welfare of all.

- *Helen Keller, 1880-1968, American Blind/Deaf Author and Lecturer*

Histories make men wise; poets, witty; the mathematics, subtle; natural philosophy, deep; moral, grave; logic and rhetoric, able to contend.

- *Francis Bacon, 1561-1626, British Philosopher/Essayist/Statesman*

Music expresses that which cannot be said and on which it is impossible to be silent. –

-*Victor Hugo, 1802-1885, French Poet/Dramatist/Novelist*

Creativity involves breaking out of established patterns in order to look at things in a different way.

- *Edward de Bono, Maltese-born Psychologist and Authority on Creative Thinking*

Better to understand a little than to misunderstand a lot.

- *Source Unknown*

A good head and a good heart are always a formidable combination.

- *Nelson Mandela, Former President of South Africa and Anti-Apartheid Activist*

The girl who can't dance says the band can't play.

- Yiddish Proverb

Happiness is like a kiss. You must share it to enjoy it.

- *Bernard Meltzer, American Law Professor*

It's not necessarily the amount of time you spend at practice that counts; it's what you put into the practice.

- *Eric Lindros, Canadian Hockey Player*

Inspiration usually comes during work, rather than before it.

- *Madeleine L'Engle, American Author and Newbery Medal Winner*

A team is where a boy can prove his courage on his own. A gang is where a coward goes to hide.

- *Mickey Mantle, 1931-1995, Hall of Fame American Baseball Player*

True love brings up everything - you're allowing a mirror to be held up to you daily.

- Jennifer Aniston, American Actress

The heart of a mother is a deep abyss at the bottom of which you will always find forgiveness.

- *Honoré de Balzac, 1799-1850, French Novelist*

Whine less, breathe more; talk less, say more; hate less, love more; and all good things are yours.

- *Swedish Proverb*

There is more to life than increasing its speed.

- *Mahatma Gandhi, 1869-1948, Indian Political and Spiritual Leader*

Stressed spelled backwards is desserts. Coincidence? I think not!

- *Source Unknown*

We are made wise not by the recollection of our past, but by the responsibility for our future.

- *George Bernard Shaw, 1856-1950, Irish Playwright and Nobel Prize Winner for Literature*

Don't ask the barber whether you need a haircut.

- *Daniel Greenberg, American Journalist*

Love the moment and the energy of that moment will spread beyond all boundaries.

- *Corita Kent, 1918-1986, American Artist and Sister of the Immaculate Heart of Mary*

Experience teaches only the teachable.

 - *Aldous Huxley, 1894-1963, British Author*

Speak when you are angry--and you will make the best speech you'll ever regret.

- *Laurence J. Peter, 1919-1988, American Educator and Writer*

Give me the ready hand rather than the ready tongue.

- *Giuseppe Garibaldi, 1807-1882, Italian Patriot and Soldier*

I've learned from experience that the greater part of our happiness or misery depends on our dispositions and not on our circumstances.

 - *Martha Washington, 1731-1802, Former First Lady of the United States*

False friendship, like the ivy, decays and ruins the walls it embraces; but true friendship gives new life and animation to the object it supports.

- *Richard Burton, 1925-1984, Welsh Actor*

Of all nature's gifts to the human race, what is sweeter to a man than his children? –

-*Marcus T. Cicero, 106-43 B.C., Great Roman Orator and Politician*

The final test of a leader is that he leaves behind him in other men the conviction and the will to carry on.

- *Walter Lippmann, 1889-1974, American Writer/Journalist/Political Commentator*

When someone is impatient and says, "I haven't got all day," I always wonder: How can that be? How can you not have all day?

 - *George Carlin, American Stand-Up Comedian and Actor*

Standing in the middle of the road is very dangerous; you get knocked down by the traffic from both sides.

- *Margaret Thatcher, Former Prime Minister of Great Britain*

The desire of knowledge, like the thirst for riches, increases ever with the acquisition of it.

- *Laurence Sterne, 1713-1768, British Author*

CHAPTER FOUR

Imagination is the highest kite that one can fly.

- Lauren Bacall, American Film and Stage Actress

Jealousy is no more than feeling alone against smiling enemies. -
-Elizabeth Bowen, 1899-1973, Irish Novelist and Short Story Writer

The measure of success is not whether you have a tough problem
to deal with, but whether it is the same problem you had last year.

*- John Foster Dulles, 1888-1959, American Statesman who served
as Secretary of State*

Ideas won't keep; something must be done about them.

*- Alfred North Whitehead, 1861-1947, British Philosopher and
Mathematician*

Nobody who ever gave his best regretted it.

- George Halas, 1895-1983, American Football Player/Coach/Owner

Disability is a matter of perception. If you can do just one thing well, you're needed by someone.

  - Martina Navratilova, Czech-born American Tennis Player

I used to say, "I sure hope things will change." Then I learned that the only way things are going to change for me is when I change.

  - Jim Rohn, American Businessman/Author/Speaker

Anger is one letter short of danger.

  - Source Unknown

Sometimes... when you hold out for everything, you walk away with nothing.
- Angela Tharp from the television series Ally McBeal, in the episode "The Promise" (originally aired on 10/27/1997)

Gratitude is the most exquisite form of courtesy.

- Jacques Maritain, 1882-1973, French Philosopher

Better three hours too soon than a minute too late.

  - William Shakespeare, 1564-1616, English Poet/Dramatist/Playwright

Reflect upon your present blessings, of which every man has plenty; not on your past misfortunes of which all men have some.

 - *Charles Dickens, 1812-1870, British Novelist*

An inventor fails 999 times, and if he succeeds once, he's in. He treats his failures simply as practice shots.

 - *Charles F. Kettering, 1876-1958, American Inventor and Engineer*

Success is not forever and failure isn't fatal.

 - *Don Shula, American Football Coach*

A man's errors are his portals of discovery.

 - *James Joyce, 1882-1941, Irish Writer and Poet*

No winter lasts forever; no spring skips its turn.

 - *Hal Borland, 1900-1978, American Writer*

Cooking is like love. It should be entered into with abandon or not at all.

 - *Harriet Van Horne, American Columnist*

An optimist laughs to forget. A pessimist forgets to laugh.

 - *Source Unknown*

If you aren't fired with enthusiasm, you will be fired with enthusiasm. -
-Vince Lombardi, 1913-1970, Hall of Fame American Football Coach

Brands are not just about fulfilling basic consumer needs. Brands possess great power and the truly great brands will be those that learn to balance this power with responsibility."

 - *Susannah Hart, John Murphy Editors, The New Wealth Creators*

"Word of mouth is the best medium of all."

- *Bill Bernbach*

"If it doesn't sell, it isn't creative."

- *David Ogilvy*

The aim of marketing is to know and understand the customer so well the product or service fits him and sells itself."

- *Peter F. Drucker*

Sustainability is here to stay or we may not be."

 - *Niall Fitzgerald, CEO Unilever*

If you can dream it, you can do it."

- *Walt Disney*

"A house of brands is like a family, each needs a role and relationship to others."

- *--Jeffrey Sinclair*

Things don't turn up in this world until somebody turns them up.

 - *James A. Garfield, 1831-1881, 20th President of the United States*

Nothing is built on stone; all is built on sand, but we must build as if the sand were stone.

- *Jorge Luis Borges, 1899-1986, Argentine Writer*

Just because a man lacks the use of his eyes doesn't mean he lacks vision.

- *Stevie Wonder, American Singer and Composer*

Do not wait for extraordinary circumstances to do good; try to use ordinary situations. –

-Jean Paul Richter, 1763-1825, German Novelist

Remember, George: No man is a failure who has friends.

- Clarence from the 1946 film "It's a Wonderful Life"

I don't wait for moods. You accomplish nothing if you do that. Your mind must know it has got to get down to work.

- Pearl S. Buck, 1892-1973, American Novelist and Pulitzer Prize Winner

Prosperity makes friends, adversity tries them.

- Publilius Syrus, 85-43 B.C., Roman Writer

Laugh at yourself first, before anyone else can.

- Elsa Maxwell, 1883-1963, American Society Hostess

Sometimes the road less traveled is less traveled for a reason.

- Jerry Seinfeld, American Actor/Writer/Comedian

It doesn't matter who my father was; it matters who I remember he was.

-Anne Sexton, 1928-1974, American Poet and Writer

Courage is being scared to death - but saddling up anyway.

- John Wayne, 1907-1979, American Movie Actor and Director

Happiness is something that comes into our lives through doors we don't even remember leaving open.

- Rose Wilder Lane, 1886-1968, American Writer and Journalist

The trick is growing up without growing old.

- Casey Stengel, 1890-1975, Hall of Fame American Baseball Manager and Player

Dreams are illustrations from the book your soul is writing about you. -
-Marsha Norman, American Dramatist and Pulitzer Prize Winner

Even a small star shines in the darkness.

- Finnish Proverb

Accept that some days you are the pigeon and some days the statue. -
-*Dilbert, American Comic Strip Engineer*

Whenever I hear, "It can't be done," I know I'm close to success. -
-*Michael Flatley, Irish-American Step Dancer*

I can't change the direction of the wind, but I can adjust my sails to always reach my destination.

 - *Jimmy Dean, American Singer/Television Performer/Sausage Entepreneur*

Old age is no place for sissies.

- *Bette Davis, 1908-1989, American Actress*

Reason often makes mistakes, but conscience never does.

 - *Josh Billings, 1815-1885, American Humorist and Lecturer*

"Home" is any four walls that enclose the right person.

- *Helen Rowland, 1875-1950, American Writer*

The man who is swimming against the stream knows the strength of it.
-Woodrow Wilson, 1856-1924, 28th President of the United States

And gain is gain, however small.

- Robert Browning, 1812-1889, English Poet and Playwright

Dreams come true; without that possibility, nature would not incite us to have them.

- -John Updike, American Novelist and Short Story Writer

Some people regard discipline as a chore. For me, it is a kind of order that sets me free to fly.

- Julie Andrews, British Actress and Singer

People should think things out fresh and not just accept conventional terms and the conventional way of doing things.

- R. Buckminster Fuller, 1895-1983, American Architect and Engineer

The universe is made of stories, not of atoms.

- Muriel Rukeyser, 1913-1980, American Poet

The art of love... is largely the art of persistence.

- Albert Ellis, American Author/Psychologist/Developer of Rational Emotive Behavioral
Therapy

A half-truth is a whole lie.

- Yiddish Proverb

Real education should educate us out of self into something far finer--into a selflessness which links us with all humanity.

- Nancy Astor, 1879-1964, English Stateswoman

Home wasn't built in a day.

- Jane Sherwood Ace, 1905-1974, American Actress and Comedienne

You've got to get up every morning with determination if you're going to go to bed with satisfaction.

- George Horace Lorimer, 1867-1937, American Editor and Writer

Comedy is simply a funny way of being serious.

- Peter Ustinov, 1921-2004, English-born Actor/Writer/Dramatist

I was always looking outside myself for strength and confidence, but it comes from within. It is there all the time.

- Anna Freud, 1895-1982, Austrian-born Psychoanalyst/Psychologist and Daughter of Sigmund Freud

You can't depend on your eyes if your imagination is out of focus.

- Mark Twain, 1835-1910, American Writer and Humorist

Remember, Ginger Rogers did everything Fred Astaire did, but she did it backwards and in high heels.

- Faith Whittlesey, Former American Ambassador to Switzerland and Aide to President Ronald Reagan

The character of a man is known from his conversations.

- Menander, 342-292 B.C., Greek Comic Dramatist

The outcome of any serious research can only be to make two questions grow where only one grew before.

- Thorstein Veblen, 1857-1929, American Economist and Social Philosopher

We must use time wisely and forever realize that the time is always ripe to do right. –

-Nelson Mandela, Former President of South Africa and Anti-Apartheid Activist

I don't want to be interesting. I want to be good.

- Ludwig Mies van der Rohe, 1886-1969, German-born Architect and Designer

Much learning does not teach understanding.

- Heraclitus, 540-480 B.C., Greek Philosopher

There must be quite a few things a hot bath won't cure, but I don't know many of them.

- Sylvia Plath, 1932-1963, American Novelist and Poet

Glory is fleeting, but obscurity is forever.

- Napoleon Bonaparte, 1769-1821, French General and Emperor

I have long since come to believe that people never mean half of what they say, and that it is best to disregard their talk and judge only their actions.

- Dorothy Day, 1897-1980, American Editor and Reformer

No trumpets sound when the important decisions of our life are made. Destiny is made known silently.

- *Agnes De Mille, 1905-1993, American Dancer and Choreographer*

CHAPTER FIVE

An optimist laughs to forget. A pessimist forgets to laugh.

 - *Source Unknown*

I know of no way of judging the future but by the past.

 - *Patrick Henry, 1736-1799, American Politician and Prominent Figure in the American Revolution*

If you aren't fired with enthusiasm, you will be fired with enthusiasm. -
-Vince Lombardi, 1913-1970, Hall of Fame American Football Coach

Comedy is simply a funny way of being serious.

 - *Peter Ustinov, 1921-2004, English-born Actor/Writer/Dramatist*

I was always looking outside myself for strength and confidence, but it comes from within. It is there all the time.

- Anna Freud, 1895-1982, Austrian-born Psychoanalyst/Psychologist and Daughter of Sigmund Freud

When you cannot make up your mind which of two evenly balanced courses of action you should take - choose the bolder.

-- W.J. Slim

All the knowledge I possess everyone else can acquire, but my heart is all my own.

- Johann Wolfgang von Goethe, 1749-1832, German Poet/Dramatist/Novelist

Don't throw stones at your neighbors, if your own windows are glass. -
- Benjamin Franklin, 1706-1790, American Scientist/Publisher/Diplomat

I only went out for a walk and finally concluded to stay out till sundown, for going out, I found, was really going in.

- John Muir, 1838-1914, Scottish-born Environmentalist and Naturalist

Runners just do it - they run for the finish line even if someone else has reached it first.

- Source Unknown

Victory belongs to the most persevering.

- Napoleon Bonaparte, 1769-1821, French General and Politician

Talk low, talk slow, and don't talk too much.

- John Wayne, 1907-1979, American Movie Actor and Director

I praise loudly. I blame softly.

- Catherine the Great, 1729-1796, Russian Empress

Be great in act, as you have been in thought.

- William Shakespeare, 1564-1616, English Poet/Dramatist/Playwright

The one sure way to success is to know everything you can about what you do.

- Donald Trump, American Businessman and Star of "The Apprentice"

True independence and freedom can only exist in doing what's right. -
-Brigham Young, 1801-1877, American Religious Leader

Failure will never overtake me if my determination to succeed is strong enough.

- Og Mandino, 1923-1996, American Motivational Author and Speaker

What we hope ever to do with ease, we must learn first to do with diligence.

- Samuel Johnson, 1709-1784, English Author and Critic

You can't really be strong until you see a funny side to things.

- Ken Kesey, 1935-2001, American Author (known for the book "One Flew Over the Cuckoo's Nest")

When placed in command - take charge.

- Norman Schwarzkopf, American General of the Gulf War

He gains everyone's approval who mixes the pleasant with the useful. -
-Horace, 65-8 B.C., Italian Poet

We can have facts without thinking but we cannot have thinking without facts.

- John Dewey, 1859-1952, American
Philosopher/Psychologist/Educational Reformer

The art of teaching is the art of assisting discovery.

- Mark Van Doren, 1894-1972, American Poet and Critic

It is above all by the imagination that we achieve perception and compassion and hope.

- Ursula K. Le Guin, American Author

Never cut what you can untie.

- Joseph Joubert, 1754-1824, French Moralist and Essayist

A man, as a general rule, owes very little to what he is born with — a man is what he makes of himself.

- Alexander Graham Bell, 1847-1922, Scottish-born Scientist and Inventor of the Telephone

You can't test courage cautiously.

- Annie Dillard, American Author

As you walk down the fairway of life you must smell the roses, for you only get to play one round.

- Ben Hogan, 1912-1997, American Golfer

The home should be the treasure chest of living.

- Le Corbusier, 1887-1965, Swiss-born Architect

My success just evolved from working hard at the business at hand each day.

- Johnny Carson, 1925-2005, American Comedian/Writer/Host of "The Tonight Show"

Fill your paper with the breathings of your heart...

- William Wordsworth, 1770-1850, British Poet

Leadership should be born out of the understanding of the needs of those who would be affected by it.

- Marian Anderson, 1897-1993, African-American Contralto

The world belongs to the enthusiast who keeps cool.

- William McFee, 1881-1966, American Author

Keep in mind that neither success nor failure is ever final.

- Roger Babson, 1875-1967, American Statistician and Entrepreneur

A man can succeed at almost anything for which he has unlimited enthusiasm.

 - Charles Schwab, 1862-1939, American Industrialist and Businessman

If you always do what interests you, at least one person is pleased.
-
-Katharine Hepburn, 1907-2003, American Film Actress

Nine tenths of education is encouragement.

- Anatole France, 1844-1924, French Author

Experience teaches slowly and at the cost of mistakes.

- James A. Froude, 1818-1894, English Historian

Success is following the pattern of life one enjoys most.

 *- Al Capp, 1909-1979, American Cartoonist (known for the satiric comic strip Li'l
Abner)*

The joy that isn't shared dies young.

- Anne Sexton, 1928-1974, American Poet and Writer

Being right half the time beats being half-right all the time.

- Malcolm S. Forbes, 1917-1990, American Publisher

I am learning all the time. The tombstone will be my diploma.

- Eartha Kitt, American Actress and Singer

Either I will find a way, or I will make one.

- Sir Philip Sidney, 1554-1586, English Poet/Courtier/Soldier

The most erroneous stories are those we think we know best - and therefore nevër scrutinize or question.

- Stephen Jay Gould, 1941-2002, American Paleontologist and Writer of Popular Science

When you make a world tolerable for yourself, you make a world tolerable
for others.

- Anais Nin, 1903-1977, French-born Author and Diarist

If a window of opportunïty appears, don't pull down the shade.

- Tom Peters, American Business Management Author and Expert

Work joyfully and peacefully, knowing that right thoughts and right efforts inevitably bring about right results.

- James Allen, 1864-1912, British-born Essayist and Author of "As a Man Thinketh"

That is the best - to laugh with someone because you both think the same
things are funny. - *Gloria Vanderbilt, American*

-Artist/Socialite/Spokeswoman for Designer Blue Jeans

If you want to be enthusiastic, act enthusiastic.

- Dale Carnegie, 1888-1955, American Author and Achievement Expert

Courage is the ladder on which all the other virtues mount.

- Clare Booth Luce, 1903-1987, American Dramatist/Journalist/Politician

No man has a good enough memory to be a successful liar.

- Abraham Lincoln, 1809-1865, 16th President of the United States

The ultimate of being successful is the luxury of giving yourself the time
to do what you want to do.

- Leontyne Price, American Opera Singer

Neither fire nor wind, birth nor death can erase our good deeds.

- *Buddha, 568-488 B.C., Founder of Buddhism*

Don't let your will roar when your power only whispers.

- *Thomas Fuller, 1608-1661, British Clergyman and Author*

I don't dream at night, I dream all day; I dream for a living.

- *Steven Spielberg, American Film Director and Producer*

You can only perceive real beauty in a person as they get older.

- *Anouk Aimee, French Actress*

Education is not the filling of a pail, but the lighting of a fire. -
-*William Butler Yeats, 1865-1939, Irish Poet/Dramatist/Mystic*

Worry gives a small thing a big shadow.

- *Swedish Proverb*

While we stop to think, we often miss our opportunity.

- *Publilius Syrus, 85-43 B.C., Roman Writer*

The universe will reward you for taking risks on its behalf.

- Shakti Gawain, American Author and Expert on Personal Growth and Consciousness

After the verb "to Love," "to Help" is the most beautiful verb in the world.

- Bertha von Suttner, 1843-1914, Austrian Novelist/Pacifist/Nobel Peace Prize Winner

Music washes away from the soul the dust of everyday life.

- Berthold Auerbach, 1812-1882, German Poet and Author

A crust eaten in peace is better than a banquet partaken in anxiety.

- Aesop, 620-560 B.C., Greek Fable Author

You have to have a dream so you can get up in the morning.

- Billy Wilder, 1906-2002, Austrian-born Film Director/Screenwriter/Producer

A real leader faces the music, even when he doesn't like the tune.

- Source Unknown

There is nothing so fatal to character as half finished tasks.

 - David Lloyd George, 1863-1945, British Statesman and Former Prime Minister of
the United Kingdom

Waste not fresh tears over old griefs.

 - Euripides, 484-406 B.C., Greek Tragic Dramatist

Don't stay in bed, unless you can make money in bed.

- George Burns, 1896-1996, American Actor and Comedian

It is good to be without vices, but it is not good to be without temptations.

- Walter Bagehot, 1826-1877, English Economist and Critic

Always borrow money from a pessimist; he doesn't expect to be paid back. -
-Source Unknown

Change is the law of life. And those who look only to the past or present are certain to miss the future.

 - John F. Kennedy, 1917-1963, 35th President of the United States

Learning is not attained by chance. It must be sought for with ardor and attended to with diligence.

- Abigail Adams, 1744-1818, Wife of United States President John Adams

CHAPTER SIX

Kites rise highest against the wind - not with it.

- *Winston Churchill, 1874-1965, British Statesman and Prime Minister*

Effective leadership is not about making speeches or being liked; leadership is defined by results not attributes.

- *Peter F. Drucker, American Management Consultant and Author*

Avoiding the phrase "I don't have time...", will soon help you to realize that you do have the time needed for just about anything you choose to accomplish in life.

- *Bo Bennett, American Businessman*

A community is like a ship; everyone ought to be prepared to take the helm.

- *Henrik Ibsen, 1828-1906, Norwegian Playwright*

Whenever you are asked if you can do a job, tell 'em, "Certainly, I can!" Then get busy and find out how to do it.

- *Theodore Roosevelt, 1858-1919, 26th President of the United States*

One of the most adventurous things left us is to go to bed. For no one can lay a hand on our dreams.

- *E.V. Lucas, 1868-1938, English Writer*

Getting ahead in a difficult profession requires avid faith in yourself. That is why some people with mediocre talent, but with great inner drive, go much further than people with vastly superior talent.

- *Sophia Loren, Italian-born Film Actress*

Next to knowing when to seize an opportunity, the most important thing in life is to know when to forego an advantage.

- *Benjamin Disraeli, 1804-1881, British Statesman and Prime Minister*

If only we'd stop trying to be happy we could have a pretty good time. -
-Edith Wharton, 1862-1937, American Novelist/Short Story Writer/Pulitzer Prize Winner

And all the loveliest things there be / Come simply, so it seems to me. -
-Edna St. Vincent Millay, 1892-1950, American Poet and Pulitzer Prize Winner

There is no cure for birth and death, save to enjoy the interval.

- George Santayana, 1863-1952, Spanish-born American Philosopher

Never a lip is curved with pain that can't be kissed into smiles again. -
-Bret Harte, 1839-1902, American Author and Poet

If a man does not keep pace with his companions, perhaps it is because he hears a different drummer. Let him step to the music which he hears, however measured or far away.

- Henry David Thoreau, 1817-1862, American Essayist/Poet/Naturalist

Fight for your opinions, but do not believe that they contain the whole truth, or the only truth.

- Charles A. Dana, 1819-1897, American Newspaper Editor

Make it a rule of life nevër to regret and nevër to look back. Regret is an appalling waste of energy; you can't build on it; it's only for wallowing in.

- Katherine Mansfield, 1888-1923, New Zealand Short Story Author

No legacy is so rich as honesty.

- William Shakespeare, 1564-1616, English Poet/Dramatist/Playwright

Reading furnishes the mind only with materials of knowledge; it is thinking that makes what we read ours.

- John Locke, 1632-1704, English Philosopher

Time is the greatest innovator.

- Francis Bacon, 1561-1626, British Philosopher/Essayist/Statesman

Life is about not knowing, having to change, taking the moment and making the best of it, without knowing what's going to happen next.

-Delicious ambiguity. - Gilda Radner, 1946-1989, American Actress and Comedienne

A good laugh is sunshine in a house.

- William Makepeace Thackeray, 1811-1863, Indian-born English Novelist

The dew of compassion is a tear.

- Lord Byron, 1788-1824, English Poet

Little minds are tamed and subdued by misfortune; but great minds rise above them. - *Washington Irving, 1783-1859, American Author*

When you see a good move, wait - look for a better one.

- *Emanuel Lasker, 1868-1941, German Chess Player and Mathematician*

The world is my country, all mankind are my brethren, and to do good is my religion. –

-*Thomas Paine, 1737-1809, English-born Pamphleteer ("Common Sense") and Founding Father of the United States*

If you have only one smile in you, give it to the people you love. Don't be surly at home, then go out in the street and start grinning 'Good morning' at total strangers.

- *Maya Angelou, American Poet and Writer*

Make voyages. Attempt them. There's nothing else.

- *Tennessee Williams, 1911-1983, American Playwright and Pulitzer Prize Winner*

There is a way to look at the past. Don't hide from it. It will not catch you if you don't repeat it.

- *Pearl Bailey, 1918-1990, American Singer and Actress*

Gratitude is not only the greatest of virtues, but the parent of all the others.

- Marcus T. Cicero, 106-43 B.C., Great Roman Orator and Politician

Oh, 'tis love, 'tis love that makes the world go round.

- The Duchess from the children's tale "Alice's Adventures in Wonderland," written by Lewis Carroll (pen name of Charles Lutwidge Dodgson)

Let us go singing as far as we go: the road will be less tedious. *- -Virgil, 70-19 B.C., Latin Poet*

A book is a gift you can open again and again.

- Garrison Keillor, American Author/Humorist/Radio Personality

The strongest of all warriors are these two--Time and Patience.

- Leo Tolstoy, 1828-1910, Russian Novelist and Philosopher

Attempt the impossible in order to improve your work.

- Bette Davis, 1908-1989, American Actress

Great minds have purposes, others have wishes.

- Washington Irving, 1783-1859, American Author

Honesty may be the best policy, but it's important to remember that apparently, by elimination, dishonesty is the second-best policy.

 - *George Carlin, American Stand-Up Comedian and Actor*

The very spring and root of honesty and virtue lie in good education. -
-Plutarch, 45-125 A.D., Greek Essayist and Biographer

Wrinkles should merely indicate where the smiles have been.

- *Mark Twain, 1835-1910, American Writer and Humorist*

People are not lazy. They simply have impotent goals -- that is, goals that do not inspire them.

- *Tony Robbins, American Author/Speaker/Peak Performänce Expert*

Nothing is a waste of time if you use the experience wisely.

- *Auguste Rodin, 1840-1917, French Sculptor*

If you lose the power to laugh, you lose the power to think.

- *Clarence Darrow, 1857-1938, American Lawyer*

Next to knowing when to seize an opportunity, the most important thing in life is to know when to forego an advantage.

Benjamin Disraeli, 1804-1881, British Statesman and Prime Minister

If only we'd stop trying to be happy we could have a pretty good time. -
-Edith Wharton, 1862-1937, American Novelist/Short Story Writer/Pulitzer Prize Winner

There is no cure for birth and death, save to enjoy the interval.

- George Santayana, 1863-1952, Spanish-born American Philosopher

Never a lip is curved with pain that can't be kissed into smiles again. -
-Bret Harte, 1839-1902, American Author and Poet

If a man does not keep pace with his companions, perhaps it is because he hears a different drummer. Let him step to the music which he hears, however measured or far away.

- Henry David Thoreau, 1817-1862, American Essayist/Poet/Naturalist

Fight for your opinions, but do not believe that they contain the whole truth, or the only truth.

 - *Charles A. Dana, 1819-1897, American Newspaper Editor*

Make it a rule of life never to regret and never to look back. Regret is an appalling waste of energy; you can't build on it; it's only for wallowing in.

- *Katherine Mansfield, 1888-1923, New Zealand Short Story Author*

The marble not yet carved can hold the form of every thought the greatest artist has. - -

-*Michelangelo, 1474-1564, Italian Renaissance Painter and Sculptor*

It's hard to lead a cavalry charge if you think you look funny on a horse.
- *Adlai Stevenson, 1900-1965, American Politician and Statesman*

The risk of a wrong decision is preferable to the terror of indecision.

-*Maimonides, 1135-1204, Spanish-born Jewish Rabbi/Physician/Philosopher*

No legacy is so rich as honesty.

- *William Shakespeare, 1564-1616, English Poet/Dramatist/Playwright*

71

Reading furnishes the mind only with materials of knowledge; it is thinking that makes what we read ours.

- John Locke, 1632-1704, English Philosopher

Time is the greatest innovator.

- Francis Bacon, 1561-1626, British Philosopher/Essayist/Statesman

Life is about not knowing, having to change, taking the moment and making the best of it, without knowing what's going to happen next. Delicious ambiguity.

- Gilda Radner, 1946-1989, American Actress and Comedienne

A good laugh is sunshine in a house.

- William Makepeace Thackeray, 1811-1863, Indian-born English Novelist

The dew of compassion is a tear.

- Lord Byron, 1788-1824, English Poet

Little minds are tamed and subdued by misfortune; but great minds rise above them.

- Washington Irving, 1783-1859, American Author

When you see a good move, wait - look for a better one.

- *Emanuel Lasker, 1868-1941, German Chess Player and Mathematician*

If you have only one smile in you, give it to the people you love. Don't be surly at home, then go out in the street and start grinning 'Good morning' at total strangers.

- *Maya Angelou, American Poet and Writer*

Make voyages. Attempt them. There's nothing else.

- *Tennessee Williams, 1911-1983, American Playwright and Pulitzer Prize Winner*

There is a way to look at the past. Don't hide from it. It will not catch you if you don't repeat it.

- *Pearl Bailey, 1918-1990, American Singer and Actress*

Gratitude is not only the greatest of virtues, but the parent of all the others.

- *Marcus T. Cicero, 106-43 B.C., Great Roman Orator and Politician*

Let us go singing as far as we go: the road will be less tedious. -
-Virgil, 70-19 B.C., Latin Poet

A book is a gift you can open again and again.

- *Garrison Keillor, American Author/Humorist/Radio Personality*

The strongest of all warriors are these two--Time and Patience.

- *Leo Tolstoy, 1828-1910, Russian Novelist and Philosopher*

Attempt the impossible in order to improve your work.

- *Bette Davis, 1908-1989, American Actress*

We should never permit ourselves to do anything that we are not willing to see our children do.

- *Brigham Young, 1801-1877, American Religious Leader*

Great ideas originate in the muscles.

- *Thomas Edison, 1847-1931, American Inventor/Entrepreneur/Founder of General Electric*

CHAPTER SEVEN

Ideas shape the course of history.

- John Maynard Keynes, 1883-1946, English Economist

Actions, not words, are the true criterion of the attachment of friends.

-George Washington, 1732-1799, 1st President of the United States

Do the thing you fear, and the death of fear is certain.

- Ralph Waldo Emerson, 1803-1882, American Poet and Essayist

With me poetry has not been a purpose, but a passion.

- Edgar Allan Poe 1809-1849, American Poet/Novelist/Short Story Writer

Wear a smile and have friends; wear a scowl and have wrinkles

- George Eliot, 1819-1880, English Female Novelist (pen name of Mary Ann Evans)

Make it a point to do something every day that you don't want to do. This is the golden rule for acquiring the habit of doing your duty without pain.

- Mark Twain, 1835-1910, American Writer and Humorist

Time is the longest distance between two places.

- Tennessee Williams, 1911-1983, American Playwright and Pulitzer Prize Winner

Eat well, drink in moderation, and sleep sound, in these three good health abound.

- Latin Proverb

The more anger towards the past you carry in your heart, the less capable you are of loving in the present.

- Barbara De Angelis, American Author and Expert on Relationships and Personal Growth

Each person must live their life as a model for others.

- Rosa Parks, 1913-2005, American Civil Rights Activist

We become just by performing just actions, temperate by performing temperate actions, brave by performing brave actions.

- *Aristotle, 384-322 B.C., Greek Philosopher*

Everything has its wonders, even darkness and silence, and I learn whatever state I may be in, therein to be content.

- *Helen Keller, 1880-1968, American Blind/Deaf Author and Lecturer*

Not in the shouts and plaudits of the throng, but in ourselves are triumph and defeat.

- *Henry Wadsworth Longfellow, 1807-1882, American Poet*

Love takes off masks that we fear we cannot live without and know we cannot live within.

- *James Baldwin, 1924-1987, American Author*

The most important thing I have learned over the years is the difference between taking one's work seriously and taking one's self seriously. The first is imperative, and the second disastrous.
-- *Margaret Fontey*

I learn by going where I have to go.
 - *Theodore Roethke*

Don't pray when it rains if you don't pray when the sun shines.
- *Satchel Paige*

Luck always seems to be against the man who depends on it.
- *Unknown*

"What lies behind us and what lies before us are tiny matters compared to what lies within us."
-- *Ralph Waldo Emerson*

I left prison more informed than when I went in. And the more informed you are, the less arrogant and aggressive you are."
--*Nelson Mandela*

True success is overcoming the fear of being unsuccessful."
- *Paul Sweeney*

Man is so made that whenever anything fires his soul, impossibilities vanish. -
-- *Jean de la Fontaine*

Talent hits a target no one else can hit; genius hits a target no one else can see."
-- *Arthur Schopenhauer*

If I'd asked my customers what they wanted,   they would have said a faster horse."
- *Henry Ford*

The wisdom of life consists in the elimination of nonessentials.
- Lin Yutang

To enforce the lies of the present, one must erase the truths of the past."
-*George Orwell*

"Those who cannot remember the past are condemned to repeat it."
-Edmund Burke

What we must decide is perhaps how we are valuable, rather than how valuable we are."
-- F. Scott Fitzgerald

"It's not what you are that holds you back. It's what you think you're not."
– Author Unknown

Many things will catch your eye. But only a few will catch your heart. Pursue them.
-- Author Unknown

"The circumstances which a person encounters with suffering are the result of his own mental inharmony. The circumstances which a person encounters with blessedness are the result of his own mental harmony
– Author Unknown

The sign of intelligent people is their ability to control emotions by the application of reason.
-- Marya Mannes (1904-1990) American Journalist

Over the years your bodies become walking autobiographies, telling friends and strangers alike of the minor and major stresses of your lives.
-- Marilyn Ferguson

Too many people overvalue what they are not and undervalue what they are.
- Malcolm Forbes

Over the years your bodies become walking autobiographies, telling friends and strangers alike of the minor and major stresses of your lives.?
- *Marilyn Ferguson*

Competence is key to ability, and credibility is key to influencing others.
– *Author Unknown*

I don't think much of a man who is not wiser today than he was yesterday
- *Abraham Lincoln*

If what you did yesterday still looks big to you, then you haven't done much today.
- *Elbert Hubbard*

It is the capacity to develop and improve their skills that distinguishes leaders from followers.
- *Warren Bennis*

An investment in your growth is an investment in your ability, your adaptability and your promotability.

– *Author Unknown*

You can change Where you started, but you can change the direction you are going.

- *Napoleon Hill*

Sometimes it is not how hard you row the boat, it is how fast the stream is going

- *Warren Buffet*

You do not lead by hitting people over the head, that's an assult

-President Dwight Eisenhower

If you keep repeating yourself after your point is made, you are just trying to get your own view.

-Anonymous

Trying to win your point at all cost with your boss can be like trying to do same with your spouse. Even if you win, you loose.

-Anonymous

To be right too soon is to be wrong

- *Emperor Hadrian*.

The glory of friendship is not in the outstretched hand, nor the kindly smile, nor the joy of companionship; it is in the spiritual inspiration that comes to one when he discovers that someone else believes in him and is willing to trust him.

– *Author Unknown*

To be capable of steady friendship or lasting love, are the two greatest proofs, not only of goodness of heart, but of strength of mind.

- *William Hazlitt*

Vision without Execution is hallucination."
– Albert Einstein

In the final analysis, it is not what you do for your children but what you have taught them to do for themselves that will make them successful human beings

– Ann Landers

Should you find yourself in a chronically leaking boat, energy devoted to changing vessels is likely to be more productive than energy devoted to patching leaks.

– Warren Buffet

Constant repetition carries conviction.

-Robert Collier

A wise man knows everything. A smart man everyone. A successful man
knows both.

-- Ancient Chinese Proverb

Brands are not just about fulfilling basic consumer needs. Brands possess great power and the truly great brands will be those that learn to balance this power with responsibility."

- *Susannah Hart, John Murphy (Editors, The New Wealth Creators)*

"What should a brand leader advertise? Brand leadership, of course. Leadership is the single most important motivating factor in consumer behavior."

- *Al Ries & Laura Ries*

"Success is not final, failure is not fatal: it is the courage to continue that counts."

- *Winston Churchill*

It is not a matter of what is true that counts, but a matter of what is perceived to be true."

- *Henry Kissinger*

Victory belongs to the most persevering."

- *Napoleon Bonaparte*

Products, like people, have personalities, and they can make or break them in the marketplace." -

- *David Ogilvy*

When dealing with people, let us remember we are not dealing with creatures of logic. We are dealing with creatures of emotion, creatures bristling with prejudices and motivated by pride and vanity."
-*Dale Carnegie*

History is the memory of things said and done."

- *Carl L. Becker*

"There are a terrible lot of lies going about the world, and the worst of it is that half of them are true."
 - *Winston Churchill*

Brands are the rock stars of commerce, and create many fans, both at home and abroad."

- *Simon Anholt, (Brand New Justice)*

Price is what you pay. Value is what you get."

- *Warren Buffett*

 It takes a big idea to attract the attention of consumers and get them to buy your product... I doubt if more than one campaign in a hundred contains a big idea."

- *David Ogilvy*

CHAPTER EIGHT

Books, the children of the brain.

- Jonathan Swift, 1667-1745, English Essayist/Novelist/Satirist

If an ad campaign is built around a weak idea - or as is so often the case, no idea at all - I don't give a damn how good the execution is, it's going to fail."

- Morris Hite

Good tactics can save even the worst strategy. Bad tactics will destroy even the best strategy."
-General George S. Patton, Jnr.

There ain't no rules around here! We're trying to accomplish something!"

-Thomas Edison

For every complex problem there is a simple solution that is wrong."
-George Bernard Shaw

The consumer isn't a moron. She is your wife."

– David Ogilvy

Unless your advertising is built on a big idea, it will pass like a ship in the night." –

-David Ogilvy

The future's already arrived; it's just not evenly distributed yet."

- William Gibson

Marketing is too important to be left to the marketing department."

-David Packard

A great brand is a story that's never completely told."

- Scott Bedbury

In a knowledge economy, a good business is a community with a purpose, not a piece of property."
-Charles Handy

Imagination is more important than knowledge."

-*Albert Einstein*

Change is the law of life. And those who look only to the past or present are certain to miss the future."
-*John F. Kennedy*

If this business were split up, I would give you the land and bricks and mortar, and I would take the brands and trademarks, and I would fare better than you."

-*John Stewart, Former CEO, Quaker*

When you reach for the stars, you may not quite get one, but you won't come up with a handful of mud either."

-*Leo Burnett*

"... money is made by discounting the obvious and betting on the unexpected."

-*George Soros*

Our company has, indeed, stumbled onto some of its new products. But never forget that you can only stumble if you are moving."

-*Richard P. Carlton, Former CEO, 3M Corporation*

Nothing strengthens the judgment and quickens the conscience like individual responsibility."

-Elizabeth Cady Stanton

The ability to learn faster than your competitors may be the only sustainable competitive advantage."
-Arie De Geus, Head of Planning, Royal Dutch Shell

Because its purpose is to create a customer, the business has two basic functions: marketing and innovation. Marketing and innovation produce results, all the rest are costs."

- Peter Drucker

The best way to predict the future is to create it."

-Peter Drucker

Don't judge each day by the harvest you reap, but by the seeds you plant."

-Robert Louis Stevenson

Almost all quality improvement comes via simplification of design, manufacturing, layout, processes, and procedures."

-Tom Peters

"Opportunity is missed by most because it is dressed in overalls and looks like work."

--- *Thomas Edison*

Leaders keep their eyes on the horizon, not just the bottom line."

- *Warren G. Bennis*

A brand is a living entity - and it is enriched or undermined cumulatively over time, the product of a thousand small gestures."

- *Michael Eisner, CEO, Disney*

Nothing is more dangerous than an idea when it's the only one you have."

- *Emile Chartier*

If everyone is thinking alike, then no one is thinking."

- *Benjamin Franklin*

Marketing is the custodian of the physical brand, but who are the custodians of behavior? If it is just HR, you've perhaps got a problem because often HR departments have lost their punch at board level. The best sponsor for an internal culture is the CEO."

- *Ian Buckingham, Interbrand Inside*

To accomplish great things, we must not only act, but also dream; not only plan, but also believe."

-Anatole France

"... even those deaf to the bragging cries of the marketplace will listen to a friend."

-Paddi Lund

"If each of us hires people who are smaller than we are, we shall become a company of dwarfs. But if each of us hires people who are bigger than we are, we shall become a company of giants."

-David Ogilvy

"Imagination rules the world."

-Napoleon Bonaparte

"Skate to where the puck is going, not where it is."

-Wayne Gretsky ice hockey legend

"An invasion of armies can be resisted, but not an idea whose time has come."

-Victor Hugo

"... if it's not your style to stretch and go the extra mile to make sure our customer experience is great, you're going to have an allergic reaction to this company. You probably won't stay. If you do try and stay, but can't adapt to the culture then it will reject you like a virus from a healthy immune system."
-Jeff Bezos

"... our first priority should be the people who work for the companies, then the customers, then the shareholders. Because if the staff are motivated then the customers will be happy, and the shareholders will then benefit through the company's success."

-Richard Branson

"You can't build a reputation on what you are going to do."

- Henry Ford

The victorious strategist only seeks battle after the victory has been won, whereas he who is destined to defeat first fights and afterwards looks for victory."

-Sun Tzu (The Art of War)

I would not give a fig for the simplicity this side of complexity, but I would give my life for the simplicity on the other side of complexity."

-Judge Oliver Wendell Holmes

"We slip from our obligation to know what consumers are thinking... into believing they are like us; and from there we slide further into believing we can think for them and understand their actions."

-William McComb

We're not concerned about having consistency of brand so much as about consistency of purpose that flows throughout the whole organization. It doesn't actually matter what we write on the napkins or say through advertising, all that matters is that when you go into a Pret shop you get that set of experiences that describes Pret."

-Andrew Rolfe, Pret A Manger

Good ideas are not adopted automatically. They must be driven into practice with courageous patience."
-Admiral Rickover

Wherever you see a successful business, someone once made a courageous decision."

-Peter F. Drucker

A business exists because the consumer is willing to pay you his money. You run a business to satisfy the consumer. That isn't marketing. That goes way beyond marketing."

- Peter F. Drucker

"If we took the mission statements of 100 large industrial companies, mixed them up while everyone was asleep, and reassigned them at random, would anyone wake up tomorrow and cry, 'My gosh, where has our mission statement gone?'"

-Hamel and Prahalad

We embarked on consciously building Virgin into a brand which stood for quality, value, fun and a sense of challenge. We also developed these ideas in the belief that our first priority should be the people who work for the companies, then the customers, then the shareholders. Because if the staff are motivated then the customers will be happy, and the shareholders will then benefit through the company's success.
-Richard Branson

"You don't build it for yourself. You know what people want and you build it for them."

- Walt Disney

If you only give people what they already want, someone else will give them what they never dreamed possible."

-Saatchi & Saatchi

Ultimately, strong branding is not just a promise to our customers, to our partners, to our shareholders and to our communities; it is also a promise to ourselves... in that sense, it is about using a brand as a beacon, as a compass, for determining the right actions, for staying the course, for evolving a culture, for inspiring a company to reach its full potential."

-Carly Fiorina CEO, Hewlett-Packard

It has always seemed to me that your brand is formed primarily, not by what your company says about itself, but what the company does."

-Jeff Bezos

"I am irresistible, I say, as I put on my designer fragrance. I am a merchant banker, I say, as I climb out of my BMW. I am a juvenile lout, I say, as I down a glass of extra strong lager. I am handsome, I say, as I don my Levi's jeans."

-John Kay Economist

"I have found the most important thing to do is decide what you're about, decide who you are, what you hold as important, and what you value. Make sure that whatever you're doing about becoming more of what you really are and not about plans and strategies that have financial gain as the starting point."

-Scott Livengood Chairman, CEO, Krispy Kreme

Any CEO who cannot clearly articulate the intangible assets of his brand and understand its connection to customers, is in trouble. "

-Charlotte Beers US Under Secretary of State

If all Coca Cola's assets were destroyed overnight , whoever owned the Coca Cola name could walk into a bank the next day morning and get a loan to rebuild everything."

-Carlton Curtis VP Corporate Communications, Coca Cola

"...nothing is so powerful as an insight into human nature, what compulsions drive a man, what instincts dominate his action, even though his language so often camouflages what really motivates him.
For if you know these things about a man you can touch him at the core of his being."
-Bill Bernbach

CHAPTER NINE

Leap and the net will appear."

-Julia Cameron

"It is a struggle to preserve a brand's aura of authenticity when layers of management, paid advertising, and unabashed promotion are added to the marketing mix. Small businesses have a distinct advantage in fostering consumer trust (and thereby boosting sales) simply by revealing their company's brand character and personality - cracks, quirks, and all."

-Kirsten Osolind

"A good product is not enough to provide competitive advantage. Only brands can tap into the emotional needs of consumers and create a bond with them."

-Jamie Lord

Singleness of purpose is one of the chief essentials for success in life, no matter what may be one's aim."

-John D. Rockefeller, Jr. 1874

Regard your good name as the richest jewel you can possibly be possessed of - for credit is like fire; when once you have kindled it you may easily preserve it, but if you once extinguish it, you will find it an arduous task to rekindle it again. The way to gain a good reputation is to endeavor to be what you desire to appear."

-Socrates

The best and most effective brands of the future will be built around knowledge."

-Lord Puttnam CBE

"We are so busy measuring public opinion that we forget we can mold it. We are also busy listening to statistics we forget we can create them."

-Bill Bernbach

"Where absolute superiority is not attainable, you must produce a relative one at the decisive point by making skillful use of what you have."

-Karl von Clausewitz (On War)

What people in business think they know about the customer and market is likely to be more wrong than right...the customer rarely buys what the business thinks it sells him." -*Peter Drucker*

The real success story of branding in recent decades has been the way in which companies have used their brands to turn the satisfaction of complex and even spiritual needs into commercial transactions."
-*Simon Anholt*

Your most unhappy customers are your greatest source of learning."

-*Bill Gates*

It is insight into human nature that is the key to the communicator's skill. For whereas the writer is concerned with what he puts into his writings, the communicator is concerned with what the reader gets out of it. He therefore becomes a student of how people read or listen."

Bill Bernbach

Your brand's power lies in dominance. It is better to have 50% of one market, instead of 10% of five markets."

-*Al Ries*

You have to live with your product, you have to know it through and through, you have to look at it, understand it, love it then, and only then, you can crystallize in one clear thought, one single theme, what must be conveyed about the product to the consumer."

-Bill Bernbach

"We are what we repeatedly do. Excellence, then, is not an act, but a habit."

-Aristotle

"There is nothing more difficult to carry out, nor more doubtful of success than to initiate a new order of things. For the reformer has enemies in all those who profit by the old order."

-Niccolo Machiavelli

Any damn fool can put on a deal but it takes genius, faith, and perseverance to create a brand."
-David Ogilvy

The secret to our enduring brand lies in delivering an experience rather than just a collection of products and services."

-Harley-Davidson annual report

Positioning is not about finding what the market wants you to be, but about finding out what you are and owning that space."

-F. Byron Nahser

The more complicated the world gets, the more comforting the familiar will seem, and the better it will get for brands."

-Fortune Magazine

We don't ask consumers what they want. They don't know. Instead we apply our brain power to what they need, and will want, and make sure we're there, ready."

-Akio Morita Sony Corporation

Quality is remembered long after the price is forgotten".

-Gucci family motto

Have regard for your name, since it will remain for you longer than a great store of gold".
-The Apocrypha

The more complicated the world gets, the more comforting the familiar will seem, and the better it will get for brands."

-Fortune Magazine

What's the reason to trust a company in a new country or in a new business it knows nothing about? My god, it's the brand."

-Laurel Cutler

You can say the right thing about a product and nobody will listen. You've got to say it in such a way that people will feel it in their gut. Because if they don't feel it, nothing will happen."

-Bill Benbach

Standing in the middle of the road is very dangerous; you get knocked down by traffic from both sides."
-Margaret Thatcher

Think small and act small, and we'll get bigger. Think big and act big, and we'll get smaller."
-Herb Kelleher

It is not the strongest of the species that survive, nor the most intelligent, but the one most responsive to change".

-Charles Darwin

"...in the factory we make cosmetics, in the store we sell hope."

-Charles Revlon

If you ever have the good fortune to create a great advertising campaign, you will soon see another agency steal it. This is irritating, but don't let it worry you; nobody has ever built a brand by imitating somebody else's advertising."

-David Ogilvy (Confessions of an Advertising Man)

Managing brands is going to be more and more about trying to manage everything that your company does."

-Lee Clow

Behind good brands lie stakeholder companies."

-Will Hutton

Never give in - never, never, never, never, in nothing great or small, large or petty, never give in except to convictions of honour and good sense. Never yield to force; never yield to the apparently overwhelming might of the enemy."

-Winston Churchill

Simplicity is all. Simple logic, simple arguments, simple visual images. If you can't reduce your argument to a few crisp words and phrases, there's something wrong with your argument. There's nothing long-winded about 'Liberté, égalité, fraternité'."

-Maurice Saatchi M&C Saatchi

We all know that the Disney brand is our most valuable asset. It is the sum total of our seventy-five years in business, of our reputation, of everything that we stand for."

-Michael Eisner, Chairman and Chief Executive, Disney

"Really strong brands are the ones that have done all my thinking for me."

-Marieke van der Werf Founder, New Moon communications agency

"A business that makes nothing but money is a poor kind of business."

-Henry Ford

The product that will not sell without advertising will not sell profitably with advertising."

-Albert Lasker

On the average, five times as many people read the headline as read the body copy. When you have written your headline, you have spent eighty cents out of your dollar."

-David Ogilvy

If I had thought about it, I wouldn't have done the experiment. The literature was full of examples that said you can't do this." (On the work that led to the unique adhesives for 3-M 'Post-It' Notepads.)
-Spencer Silver

Knowledge is a process of piling up facts; wisdom lies in their simplification."

-Alexander Graham Bell

The essence of positioning is sacrifice. You must be willing to give up something in order to establish that unique position."

-Al Ries & Jack Trout (Positioning: The Battle for your Mind)

To swear off making mistakes is very easy. All you have to do is swear off having ideas.

- " Leo Burnett

"Looking at small advantages prevents great affairs from being accomplished."

-Confucius

Normally, I am not a betting man but on one thing I've bet more than US$18 billion in the last three years my belief that the future of consumer goods marketing belongs to the companies with the strongest brands."

-Hamish Maxwell, Phillip Morris

Advertising promotes that divine discontent which makes people strive to improve their economic status."

-Ralph S. Butler

Give people a taste of Old Crow, and tell them it's Old Crow. Then give them another taste of Old Crow, but tell them it's Jack Daniels. Ask them what they prefer. They'll think the two drinks are different. They are testing images."

-David Ogilvy, Ogilvy on Advertising

In times of change, learners inherit the Earth, while the learned find themselves beautifully equipped to deal with a world that no longer exists."

-Anon

The ultimate test of a moral society is the kind of world it leaves to its children

– Dietrich Bonhoeffer

You have only 30 seconds [in a TV commercial]. If you grab attention in the first frame with a visual surprise, you stand a better chance of holding the viewer. People screen out a lot of commercials because they open with something dull ... When you advertise fire-extinguishers, open with the fire."

-David Ogilvy

Doing business without advertising is like winking at a girl in the dark. You know what you're doing, but nobody else does."

-Stuart H. Britt

Remember that there is nothing stable in human affairs; therefore avoid undue elation in prosperity, or undue depression in adversity.

- Socrates

When it comes to life the critical thing is whether you take things for granted or take them with gratitude.

- G. K. Chesterton

Everything that exists is in a manner the seed of that which will be.

--Marcus Aurelius

If everybody is thinking alike, then somebody isn't thinking

– *George S Patton*

Isn't it unnerving that doctors call what they do 'practice'?"

 – *George Carlin*

CHAPTER TEN

Be yourself. Everyone else is already taken

- Oscar Wilde

He who rejects change is the architect of decay. The only human institution which rejects progress is the cemetery.

-Harold Wilson

Peace is not something you wish for; It's something you make,

Something you do, Something you are, And something you give away.

-- Robert Fulghum

The possibilities are numerous once we decide to act and not react.

- George Bernard Shaw quotes

Always remember to slow down in life; live, breathe, and learn; take a look around you whenever you have time and never forget everything and every person that has the least place within your heart.

– *Anonymous*

I'd rather have a moment of wonderful than a lifetime of nothing special.

-- *Author Unknown*

Getting in touch with your true self must be your first priority.

-*Tom Hopkins*

When I stand before God at the end of my life, I would hope that I would not have a single bit of talent left, and could say, "I used everything you gave me."

~*Erma Bombeck*

If you treat people right, they will treat you right -- at least 90 percent of the time."

– *Franklin Delano Roosevelt*

'Our lives are better left to chance. I could have missed the pain, but I'd have had to miss the dance.'

-Garth Brooks song:

I start with the premise that the function of leadership is to produce more leaders, not more followers."

– Ralph Nader

The work will wait while you show the child the rainbow, but the rainbow won't wait while you finish the work.

- Pat Clifford

Everything has been said before, but since nobody listens we have to keep going back and beginning all over again."
 -- Andre Gide

It's easier to act your way into a new way of thinking than to think your way into a new way of acting."

– Monique Sternin

If the rich could hire other people to die for them, the poor could make a wonderful living.

– Yiddish Proverbs

It is impossible to defeat an ignorant man in an argument

— *William Gibbs McAdoo*

There are two kinds of failures; those who thought and never did
and those who did and never thought

— *Laurence J. Peter*

All the good maxims have been written - it only remains to put
them into practice

— *Blaise Pascal*

Civilization is nothing more than the effort to reduce the use of
force to the last resort."

— *Jose Ortegay Gasset*

Chains of habit are too light to be felt until they are too heavy to be
broken"

— *Warren Buffet*

Risk comes from not knowing what you're doing"

— *Warren Buffet*

Do not go where the path may lead, go instead where there is no path and leave a trail"

– Ralph Waldo Emerson

Not to be suspicious in the world of men is not only naïve, it is irresponsible"

– Howard Jacobson

There are two primary choices in life: to accept conditions as they exist, or accept the responsibility for changing them."
- Denis Waitley

If you think you're too small to have an impact, try going to bed with a mosquito

– Anita Roddick

Just remember, once you're over the hill you begin to pick up speed."

– Charles Schulz

The quality of life is in the mind, not in material.

The world is filled with beauty when your heart is filled with love.

We grow because we struggle, we learn, and we overcome.

Goodness is the only investment that never fails.

You can plant a dream.

Live every day of your life as though you expect to live forever.

Don't believe in miracle - depend on them.

Kind words do not cost much, yet they accomplish much.

Cherish yesterday, dream tomorrow, and live today.

Be not simply good, but good for something.

Happiness is not pleasure, it is victory.

To desire is to obtain, to aspire is to achieve.

To have character is to be big enough to take life on.